# COUNTING to 17

J2B Publishing,
4251 Columbia Park Road, Pomfret, MD 20675
www.J2BLLC.com
202-557-8097


Cover Art and Design by Mary Barrows
Interior Design by Mary Barrows

Book is set in Garamond

ISBN: 978-1-948747-25-7

# COUNTING
## to 17

A.E. Peremel

J2B PUBLISHING

*Dedicated to the 17 dead and 14 injured
in the Parkland, Florida school shooting,*

*Never Again*

# Introduction

I am an eighth grade student in Annapolis, Maryland. I was in the seventh grade at the time of the shootings in Marjory Stoneman Douglas High School in Parkland, Florida, that left 17 dead and 14 wounded.

There have been so many shootings over the past year and I made it my duty to check regularly whether there was one. I wondered why was their life taken, instead of my own?

I quickly realized that I can't just sit back and watch the shootings as they seem to become more and more frequent and more and more people give up hope. I can't continue on with my life, acting like everything is ok when I can make a change.

I decided to write about the shooting and donate all profits from this book to making schools safer. Donations will be sent to **Americans for Children's Lives and School Safety** found at www.americansforclass.org.

# One

Not many people can say that they lived through a school shooting

I can't say that I have

But maybe the reason some people can't say that they lived through one

Is because they didn't really *live* through it

It's hard to imagine the air thick with bullets

Blood splattered against the window panes

Quiet victims taking their final breaths

I can't say that I lived through one

But I also can't say that the shooting didn't change me

17, 17, 17

The number bounces around my mind

It is no longer the number after 16, before 18

It is the number of death

Carnage

Regret

Could have beens

Still echoing the forgotten futures of the dead

# Two

Alyssa Alhadeff, 14 - Talented

Martin Duque Anguiano, 14 - Sweet

Scott Beigel, 35 - Alive

Nicholas Dworet, 17 - Connected

Aaron Feis, 37 - Hero

Jaime Guttenberg, 14 - Friend

Chris Hixon, 49 - Father

Luke Hoyer, 15 - Cherished

Cara Loughran, 14 - Grace

Gina Montalto, 14 - Angel

Joaquin Oliver, 17 - Blessing

Alaina Petty, 14 - Vibrant

Meadow Pollack, 18 - Beautiful

Helena Ramsay, 17 - Warmth

Alex Schachter, 14 - Melodic

Carmen Schentrup, 16 - Scholar

Peter Wang, 15 - Smile

# Three

Fear

Paranoia

Panic

Words thrown around as if they mean nothing

Yet nobody is truly able to understand their meanings

Not even in the face of death

Tears running red

Do we really know what fear is?

Not even when the world seems against us

Strange men at every corner

Do we really know what paranoia is?

And not even pulling a trigger

Voices in your head compelling you

Do we really know what panic is?

What we know are the echoes of the past

Of people who claim to know those feelings

But really, the only people that knew, will never be able to say

# Four

What is your biggest fear?

Is it death?

Is it pain?

Is it grief?

Is it loss?

Is it Spiders?

Or heights?

Or Isolation?

What about fire?

Is it that that you don't belong?

Or that you never will?

Is it dying unfairly?

Or dying a coward?

A person that you can't trust?

Maybe *The Boy With The Gun*?

Everybody has a reason to fear him

Especially when you are the one that his gun is pointed at

# Five

If your life flashed before your eyes,

What would you see?

Would what you see

Impress you?


Final cries ring out

The green lawn

Stained with blood

A place for learning

Now a graveyard

For the wronged dead

Full of sins

And regrets


If your life flashed before your eyes

Would you think about the future?

Or the past?

One day, we will all watch the blue sky fade away

Soon to be one with the dust

# Six

N**ger

          B**ch

    Dumb ass

              Jerk

      Ugly

                 Corrupt

            Retard

                    Worthless

Words all thrown around

In today's society

All taken back

With

    One

      Final

      Breath

When the people are gone

Their words are still remembered

# Seven

Survivors

      Bloody

Ailing

      Dying

Wailing sirens

      Hurrying down busy streets

Life continues on like normal

      But for some

Life won't be continuing

      One gunshot

And then another

      31 people

Hit by flying bullets

      Breaking the order of a

Busy classroom

      Leaving others alive

But broken

# Eight

Shouts ring out

Louder than the gunshots

That

   Follow

Bullets flying through the air

Like missiles

Each one locked on a target

Everything slows

31 bodies

Barely breathing

Triumphant tyrant

Captured, but too late

Doesn't know that he, too

Is as good

As dead

People who will never live

To see their killer

# Nine

Everybody is fighting their own battle

Each person their own story

Every human their own conflict

Sometimes we fight our battles against

Another person

A law

A community

But sometimes we fight the battles

Against ourselves

What were the victims thinking?

As they drew their last breath

Did it come easy?

Their battles surrendered?

Or did it come painfully?

All 17 of them trying to finally win

And all 17 of them killed by *The Man With The Gun*

Their battles forgotten

# Ten

Ordinary people

Getting ready for school

Saying goodbye to their families

Just like every other ordinary day

Not knowing that

They will never return home

17 ordinary families

Scarred and broken

In ways that can never

Be

Fixed

Because of one human

Who some call sick

Others call evil

And more call demented

But no ordinary word

Can describe how truly wrong he was

# Eleven

When in life do you say your last goodbye?

Will you be old and prosperous?

Young but happy?

What about when you're 14?

When there is still a whole world to explore?

Each victim said their last goodbye

Expecting to say another, tomorrow

Each one of us

Saying goodbye

And returning home safely

What about the day that we never return home?

Nobody lives forever

But would forever even be long enough

For us to say our final goodbye?

Nobody is truly ready for death

To take our last breath

To say farewell to this beautiful world

# Twelve

They say that everybody is equal

But can that be true?

If one man holds power over another

A gun trained on a child's face

Is that child still equal to the one

Holding the gun?

He can pull the trigger at any moment

And this child

Would be dead

Their cold boy sprawled against the floor

Blood stained hair

Glazed eyes

Is that child

Still equal

To the man

That pulled

The trigger?

# Thirteen

, a pause, as the gun is pointed

At the victims head

: the bullet finds its mark

. for them, it is over

; for some, life will go on

... for others, the future is uncertain

# and many, will never get a choice

( ) for the whispers of the past

* for the echoes of the future

" for the ones who no longer have a voice

' and for those who never will

- for those who died young

[ ] and those who gave their lives

; for some, life will go on

... for others, the future is uncertain

# and many will never get a choice

. for them, it is over

*Note: The point of the symbols and punctuation marks before each phrase is just another way to tell the story. You don't always need words, because sometimes, they aren't enough.*

# Fourteen

We say never again

Yet every child still fears

*The Man With The Gun*

We say never forget

Yet each day

The past slips through our fingers

More and more

We try to learn from our mistakes

But people still die

At the hands of madmen

We know that history repeats itself

Yet we don't know how to keep it from doing so

We try and change the world

But one person isn't enough to change it

We need the violence to stop

And that starts with every single

One of us

# Fifteen

One bullet

Is enough to quiet laughter

Hush tears

Change someone's life

And end another

One bullet

Is enough to alter the future

Freeze the past

Destroy a community

Ruin a school

One bullet

Is enough to make a country rebel

To tear apart a family

To silence a friend

To change the world

One bullet

Is enough to end a life

# Sixteen

Five years from now

The names of the victims will be forgotten

Ten years from now

Nobody will remember exactly what happened

And in 20 years the memories will be disregarded

The event forgotten

Lost in the sea of the past

A relic of time

But some will always remember

The ones that watched the bullets race towards their target

The ones that watched their friends drown in pools of blood

They are burdened with remembering

When all they want to do is forget

Why should we let these victims' identities fade into the past?

Why are they any less deserving than us?

We can try to move on

But we must never forget

# Seventeen

In Stoneman Douglas High School

Blood still runs down the window panes

Screams still ring through the halls

And the echoes of the past

Live on

In the voices of the future


In Stoneman Douglas High School

17 students will never graduate

14 will have their scars for the rest of their lives

And 100s of students have wounds

That go deeper than the bullets that caused them


In Stoneman Douglas Highschool

These 17 victims will never be forgotten

Their stories will never be disregarded

Just because they are dead doesn't mean they are gone

Just because their voices are silent

Doesn't mean the echoes aren't there

# Author's Note

You may have noticed that each poem has 17 lines, which is 289 lines in total; that's around 11 pages. As an amateur author, I could write that much in a day or two. But it still took me eight months to finish these poems. I didn't want to sit there and write them, I wanted to feel them. It's not the same unless the poem comes to you. Throughout these past eight months, I realized how much the shooting really did change me. How the deaths of 17 strangers, could really affect me.

I know that these 289 lines won't change the world, but maybe they will change your mind. We all have a voice for a reason and I'm using mine, to help you find yours.

As Mahatma Gandhi once said, *"Be the change that you wish to see in the world."*

It really does start with every single one of us.

www.ingramcontent.com/pod-product-compliance
Lightning Source LLC
Chambersburg PA
CBHW070750050426
42449CB00010B/2413